Contents

Preface

The development of relations among the United States, China, and Japan will significantly shape the future of the Asia-Pacific region and the international order of the 21st century. The three countries rank first, second, and third, respectively, in gross domestic product among the world's economies. In terms of economic interdependence and mutual benefit, each has strong incentives to cooperate and to structure "win-win" outcomes. At the same time, China's reemergence as a dynamic force both within the Asia-Pacific region and beyond, perhaps with a distinct view of incentives and national interests, is a reality facing both the United States and Japan. This study looks at the structure of and the challenges inherent in the relationship between Asia's two great neighboring powers, China and Japan.

Acknowledgments

I want to thank my colleagues—both past and present—in the Center for Strategic Research, Institute for National Strategic Studies, at the National Defense University, in particular Renata Louie, Mark Redden, Nicholas Rostow, Ferial Saeed, and Phillip Saunders, for their support, encouragement, and well-directed critiques that contributed to the writing of this paper.

Executive Summary

Between China and Japan, the past is ever-present. Notwithstanding shared cultural and historic ties, throughout the past century and going back to the Sino-Japanese war at the end of the 19ᵗʰ century, a bitter legacy of history—the Boxer Rebellion; the Mukden Incident and Japan's occupation of South Manchuria (1931); the Marco Polo Bridge Incident, Japan's subsequent invasion of China, and the Nanjing Massacre (1937); and the Sino-Japanese War (1937–1945)—has left an indelible mark on this relationship.

Nevertheless, the two countries have demonstrated the ability to put history on the back burner in order to address immediate needs. Diplomatic relations were normalized in 1972 and a Treaty of Peace and Friendship, committing the two countries to economic and political cooperation, was signed in 1978. Japan's Official Development Assistance programs and low interest yen loans contributed to the success of China's market opening reforms initiated by Deng Xiaoping.

This study examines the metafactors shaping the China-Japan relationship: the rise of China, a competition for regional leadership within a shifting balance of power, and history. At the strategic level, there is intense, but quiet, political competition for the mantle of leadership in the Asia-Pacific region. With memories of history suffusing critical aspects of the relationship, managing and adjusting to China's growing influence and successfully managing relations will challenge political leadership both in Beijing and in Tokyo.

There are also several macro-structural factors that shape the China-Japan relationship. They begin with the critically important economic relationship. In 2006, China became Japan's top trading partner, and in 2007 China became Japan's top export market, in both instances replacing the United States. Within Japan's business community, the China boom is widely recognized as the driving force behind Japan's recovery from its "lost decade" in the 1990s. The increasing integration of the two economies provides ballast to a bilateral relationship that is also marked by a number of combustible political issues including conflicting territorial claims, a disputed maritime boundary in the East China Sea, and security anxieties in both countries. As a result, there is a dynamic and shifting tension among economic, political, and security interests. In both countries, these elements add inherent volatility to the bilateral relationship within which day-to-day problems are addressed.

Finally, this study considers a number of case studies focused on the day-to-day challenge of managing issues that, if left unaddressed, could harm significant national interests on both sides of the bilateral relationship and complicate realization of the benefits of a "Mutually

Beneficial Relationship based on Common Strategic Interests." Day-to-day issues such as the East China Sea, food safety, history, and security may not lend themselves to resolution in the short- to midterm, but finding ways to deal with or work around the issues is critical to keep the relationship more or less on an even keel and moving forward. At the same time, highly nationalistic, zero-sum issues relating to sovereignty, such as the September 2010 Senkaku incident, have the potential to derail the relationship at significant cost to both parties. Across the board, issues must be managed with utmost care if Sino-Japanese relations are to reach their full potential.

Introduction

Early in this new century, issues related to history dominated the China-Japan political landscape. The visits of Prime Minister Junichiro Koizumi (2001–2006) to the Yasukuni Shrine triggered strong diplomatic protests from China and led to the breakdown of high-level contacts. In August 2004, Japan's 3-1 victory over China in the China-hosted Asian Cup prompted Chinese spectators to burn the Japanese flag, rock the Japanese team bus, and assault an embassy vehicle belonging to the Japanese minister. Chinese police kept Japanese fans inside the stadium for 2 hours after the game while they restored order outside. In April 2005, violent anti-Japanese rioting erupted in Beijing and Shanghai in response to the ministry of education's approval of a *New History Textbook*, which the Chinese viewed as a Japanese government-backed attempt to whitewash the past, and to Japan's efforts to gain a permanent seat on the United Nations Security Council. The riots were front-page news in Japan.

Since the advent of the Shinzo Abe government in September 2006, both China and Japan have worked to repair and stabilize the bilateral relationship. Prime Minister Abe's "ice-breaking" visit to China in October 2006 produced agreement on a framework for the relationship, "A Mutually Beneficial Relationship based on Common Strategic Interests," which successive Japanese governments following Abe and the Chinese administration of President Hu Jintao and Prime Minister Wen Jiabao have worked to implement. Their efforts have yielded a fragile rapprochement that made possible summit meetings and increased bilateral cooperation, in particular on economic and environmental issues as well as on North Korea, while leaving fundamental issues such as those relating to sovereignty over disputed islands unresolved and subject to nationalist passions in both countries.

Today, diplomats on both sides recognize the tentative nature of the improvement in relations. They also understand that the state of Sino-Japanese relations—and the ability of the two countries to cooperate—is significant for their respective national interests.

PART I: Metafactors: Past, Present, and Future in China-Japan Relations

There are several metafactors[1] that affect Sino-Japanese relations. They involve history, the rise of China over the past two decades, and a competition for regional leadership within a shifting balance of power. In both countries, they provide the background against which structural issues shape the relationship and ad hoc problems are addressed.

History

The legacies of history are an inextricable part of domestic politics in both China and Japan. Japan's invasion of China in the 1930s and the atrocities committed by Japanese military forces have served to fan popular resentment against Japan, aggravated by what the Chinese perceive as Japan's reluctance to accept responsibility for its wartime actions. China's sense of aggrieved nationalism, reinforced through a patriotic education campaign in the 1990s, has resulted in anti-Japanese demonstrations and, at times, the destruction of Japanese property and even physical assault on Japanese nationals and diplomatic property in China. Such occurrences are widely covered in the Japanese media and affect Japanese perceptions of China.

The anti-Japanese component of Chinese nationalism has become a double-edged sword for China's leadership. On the one hand, Japan has played a central role in Chinese nationalist myths and has frequently been used as a foil to demonstrate China's superior moral position.[2] The historical legacy and popular resentment of Japan means that anti-Japanese sentiments play well in Chinese politics and are a source of legitimacy for the Chinese government.[3] On the other hand, given internal political needs and the pragmatic challenges of managing the bilateral relationship, Beijing sometimes has had to walk a fine line between sanctioning public expressions of protest against Japan that satisfy domestic concerns and not undermining cooperative economic relations.[4]

In Japan, there is a widespread sense that China blames Japan for many of its own failings, while ignoring the responsibility of China's own communist leaders. Following President Jiang Zemin's history lecture at a state banquet in the presence of the Japanese emperor and during the Koizumi era, a strong sense that no apology would ever suffice to assuage China's sense of historical grievance prevailed in Japan. Japan provided China with billions of dollars in economic development assistance, but the Japanese have frequently asserted that China has failed to acknowledge their aid.[5] These concerns have been reinforced by the emergence of a post–World War II generation that for the most part lacks a sense of personal responsibility for Japanese actions during the war years.

At the same time, a small minority of ultranationalists have frequently minimized Japan's actions of the 1930s and 1940s. In November 2008, Toshio Tamogami, chief of staff of Japan's Air Self-Defense Force, published an award-winning essay in a contest sponsored by Toshio Motoya, a conservative businessman and publisher, who aimed to encourage essays on the theme "True Views of Modern History." Tamogami's essay argued that Japan was not an aggressor during the Pacific War but rather a victim of Chinese and American machinations. The essay produced shock and indignation in Beijing. Tamogami was relieved of command but remains a voice in Japan's political debate.

The unprecedented China-Japan Joint History 2006–2009 project, aimed at enhancing mutual understanding of the past, produced papers from individual scholars but, by agreement, no consensus view of the past. Referring to Japan's wartime aggression in China, the outline of the section dealing with modern and contemporary history acknowledged the existence of large gaps in understanding between the two peoples on "the nature of war and war responsibility."[6] Notwithstanding such efforts to address the past, both governments and societies live with the reality that strong historically rooted animosities are not far from the surface, however correct diplomatic relations and profitable business ties remain.

Present and Future: The Rise of China and Competition for Leadership

An underlying source of uncertainty in the bilateral relationship is the change in the relative balance of power between China and Japan. Over the past 150 years, there has never been a period in which China and Japan were internally united and strong—until now. During the 1970s and 1980s, Japan emerged as an economic superpower, while China, beset by the disarray of the Cultural Revolution, was only beginning to adopt the economic reforms that have produced today's remarkable growth.

Today, China's dynamic economy and its increasingly sophisticated diplomacy in East Asia and on the world stage are challenging long-held Japanese assumptions of regional leadership and international standing based on the strength of Japan's economy, which still bears the scars of the 1990s "lost decade" of economic stagnation. In January 2010, the *Asahi Shimbun* newspaper began the year with a look-ahead series, "Japan as Number 3." At the end of the year, Japan became the world's third largest economic power as China's surging economy moved it into second place behind only the United States in gross domestic product ranking. At the same time, China's economic success has fueled the modernization of the People's Liberation Army (PLA). Two decades of double-digit increases in defense spending have enhanced PLA strategic and power projection capabilities. This evolving power balance is reflected in an ongoing competition for leadership in the Asia-Pacific region and beyond.

Beijing strongly supported the work of the East Asian Study Group, which in 2002 advanced the concept of an East Asian Summit including members of the Association of Southeast Asian Nations plus China, Japan, and South Korea. Notably absent were three of Asia's democracies, Australia, India, and New Zealand, as well as the United States. Japan, along with Singapore, subsequently worked to include Australia, India, and New Zealand in what was widely perceived as an effort to balance Chinese influence.

In November 2006, Japan's Foreign Minister Taro Aso called for an Arc of Freedom and Prosperity that would extend from Northeast Asia to Central Asia and the Middle East. The Arc would be governed by "values-oriented diplomacy," with an emphasis on "universal values, such as democracy, freedom, human rights, rule of law and the market economy."[7] The initiative was widely interpreted as an effort by Japan to set the rules of the road for an Asian community, with standards that stood in stark contrast to China's practices. In 2009, when Prime Minister Yukio Hatoyama called for the establishment of an East Asian Community, Beijing's response was to express support for the concept but to remind Tokyo that China had the idea first.

This rivalry for regional leadership contrasts significantly with the European case, where Germany for decades following World War II allowed France to play a central leadership role in European politics despite Germany's greater economic weight. In the case of China and Japan, competition also colors relationships with other countries in Asia.

Japanese officials are focused on China's increasing influence within the Asia-Pacific region. Beijing's efforts to court countries affiliated with the Association of Southeast Asian Nations (ASEAN), including a China-ASEAN free trade agreement, have placed Japan in a reactive position. Yet, internal political problems related to agriculture have made it difficult for Japan to respond with an aggressive regional trade agenda of its own. Japan has been more active in proposing monetary cooperation within Asia, an arena where domestic political concerns do not play so large a role. But an unacknowledged competition for regional influence continues to mark the Japan-China relationship.

Competition is also evidenced at the United Nations (UN), where Japan, Brazil, Germany, and India have advocated expanding the number of permanent members on the UN Security Council. While supporting United Nations Security Council (UNSC) reform as a long-term objective, China has worked effectively to limit support for Japan's bid for a permanent seat. Beijing's effort was most notable with the African Union (AU). As Japanese diplomats targeted African countries that had benefited from Japan's economic assistance programs and worked to build their support for a resolution that would advance Japan's candidacy for a permanent seat, China engaged in quiet diplomacy among AU members and essentially outbid Japan with promises of future aid. The AU ultimately declined to endorse Japan's candidacy.[8] When To-kyo, along with other G-4 members (Brazil, India, Japan, and Germany), raises the question of China's support for permanent seating, Beijing's answer is to position the Security Council issue as "part and parcel of the UN reforms," with priority assigned to "increasing the representation of developing countries, African countries in particular." And comprehensive reform of the UN borders on mission nearly impossible.[9]

China also has not been averse to playing the history card regarding Japan's quest for a permanent seat on the UNSC. During a 2005 visit to India, Premier Wen announced that "only a country that respects history, takes responsibility for history and wins over the trust of the peoples of Asia and the world at large can take greater responsibilities in the international com-munity."[10] Wen's remarks came in April 2005, when anti-Japanese riots broke out in China in response to Japan's Ministry of Education approval of a New History Textbook and in response to Japan's bid to gain a permanent seat on the UNSC.

PART II: Macro-structural Factors

There are also a number of structural factors that contour and complicate the relationship. They include economic issues, geography, security concerns, and political values. The result is a dynamic and shifting tension among economic, political, and security interests. In both countries, these elements add a measure of unpredictable volatility to the bilateral relationship against which day-to-day problems are addressed.

Economic Relations: The Numbers Tell the Story

In 2006, China became Japan's top trading partner and, in 2007, China became Japan's top export market, in both instances replacing the United States. Within Japan's business community, the China boom is widely recognized as the driving force behind Japan's recovery from its "lost decade" in the 1990s. From 2000 to 2010, Japanese exports to China (mainland) grew from $30.356 billion to $149.626 billion; over the same period imports from China in-creased from $55.156 billion to $153.369 billion.[11] In the first half of 2010, Japan's total trade with China increased 34.5 percent. As Robert Alan Friedman, Morgan Stanley chief econo-mist in Tokyo, observed, "There has been acceleration of trade, and, for Japan, that's where the growth is."[12]

Despite the risks of anti-Japanese nationalism, Japanese companies have continued to move to the mainland over the past two decades. Honda, Nissan, and Toyota operate production facilities in China as joint venture partners with Chinese automobile companies. Japan and China have agreed to 44 joint venture projects involving technology transfer in the fields of energy and the environment. Japan's advertising giant Dentsu has teamed up with China's Suntrend Group; China's computer leader Lenovo has entered into a joint venture with Japan's information technology firm NEC, taking a 51 percent majority stake; and in the period January–May 2010, the Japan National Tourist Organization reported that 600,000 Chinese tourists visited Japan, an increase of 36 percent over 2009.

For Japan, increasing economic integration with China has also increased risk. The reality of risk was underscored during the Senkaku incident, when China demonstrated that it was prepared to use economic leverage to secure political objectives—the release of a fishing boat captain detained by Japan. To bring pressure to bear on the Japanese government, Beijing suspended rare earth metal exports, slowed customs clearance procedures, and issued tourist industry guidance on travel to Japan. To offset risks involved in doing business in China, many Japanese companies have adopted "China plus One" strategies, shifting investment and production facilities to Malaysia, Vietnam, and Indonesia, not in lieu of continuing to invest in China, but as a risk management strategy.

Yet integration of the two economies continues apace, positioning the economic relationship as the ultimate shock absorber in a bilateral relationship that is also marked by a number of challenging political issues.

Geography: Neighbors Divided by Territorial and Maritime Disputes

A longstanding controversy involves the Senkaku/Diaoyu Islands in the East China Sea. Both China and Japan claim sovereignty over the islands, which are currently administered by Japan. Both sides have mined the historical record for evidence to support their claims, and nationalist groups in Japan and China as well as Hong Kong and Taiwan have taken action, sometimes against government wishes, to build advocacy support.

The issue of sovereignty is directly related to the UN Convention on the Law of the Sea (UNCLOS), which establishes a 200-nautical-mile Exclusive Economic Zone (EEZ) for resource exploration and development. The legal and policy question is whether Japan's southernmost territory, Okinotorishima, is an island (as Japan asserts) from which its EEZ can be extended, or simply a rock (as Beijing asserts), unable to sustain life or economic activity and thus unable to support EEZ claims. To reinforce Japan's claim and in the face of Chinese protests, the government of Prime Minster Hatoyama initiated conservation measures on Okinotorishima to protect against soil erosion and rising sea levels; it has also earmarked funds to construct port facilities to support economic activity.

On both sides, sovereignty claims retain the flavor of the Koizumi era. During a Japan-China summit in December 2008, the Japanese press reported that there had been "heated verbal exchanges" between Prime Minister Taro Aso and Premier Wen Jiabao over ownership of the Senkaku Islands.[13] Sun Shuxian, deputy director of the China Marine Surveillance, was quoted as saying that "In sea areas where there is a territorial dispute under international law, it is important to display presence in the sea area under jurisdiction and continue accumulating records of effective control."[14] Both sides fear that any concessions might undermine their underlying claims and encourage domestic opposition.

Beijing and Tokyo are also involved in an ongoing dispute over maritime boundaries in the East China Sea. Japan supports a demarcation based on the center line principle, while China argues for a position based on the continental shelf principle, which would give China a larger EEZ extending through the Okinawa trough. Both positions have some support under UNCLOS. But the legal debate is complicated by the fact that both China and Japan are engaged in exploration of the sea bottom for potentially valuable oil and natural gas reserves. Chinese oil companies are already drilling on the Chinese side of the midline boundary, and Tokyo has complained that Chinese activities may be siphoning off reserves from the Japanese side of the disputed area.

In May 2010, the Japanese research ship *Shoyo*, while operating within Japan's claimed EEZ—that is, on the eastern side of the midline boundary—was pursued by a Chinese patrol ship and ordered to cease its activities. The Japanese ship complied but the foreign ministry protested the Chinese action on the grounds that *Shoyo* was conducting research in accordance with international law. Beijing responded that the area in question is under Chinese jurisdiction and the actions taken by the Chinese ship were totally proper and legitimate. Today, sovereignty issues and EEZ claims are a constant irritant and an ongoing source of friction in the bilateral relationship.

Security Concerns

Security concerns are also an inextricable element of the relationship and, over the past decade, have assumed a higher profile in both China and Japan.

The current bilateral military balance is inherently asymmetric.

China is a nuclear weapons state and is engaged in a military modernization program in which defense spending has increased annually at a double-digit rate for over two decades. The modernization program has improved China's power projection capabilities. Japanese analysts are concerned about China's growing submarine fleet, its expanding missile force, as well as China's stepped up exploration and intelligence gathering activities in Japan's EEZ and in international waters off Japan. There are also broader concerns about how an authoritarian Chinese government might use China's increased military capabilities in the future.

Japan, meanwhile, has forsworn the development or possession of nuclear weapons, has constitutional limits on the use military power, and has maintained a political ceiling of 1 percent of gross domestic product on its defense spending.[15] Instead, Japan has relied on its alliance with the United States. Article V of the Mutual Security Treaty commits the United States to meet "the common danger posed by an armed attack . . . in the territories under the administration of Japan." Under Article VI, "Japan grants the United States the use 'by its land, air, and naval force of facilities and areas in Japan' for the purpose of contributing to the security of Japan and the maintenance of international peace and stability in the Far East." Over the past decade, Japan has worked to strengthen its security alliance with the United States and to increase defense planning, cooperation, and coordination with the United States, particularly in the area of missile defense.

Unquestionably, the threat posed by North Korea's missiles and nuclear weapons has served to advance security cooperation with the United States, but, in private conversations, Japanese officials and security analysts also emphasize the long-term strategic challenge posed by the rise of China. Ministry of defense and Self-Defense Force (SDF) officials in particular are concerned with the impact of China's growing antiaccess/area-denial capabilities as putting at risk the U.S. forward-deployed strategy, undercutting extended deterrence, and posing an existential threat to Japan.

For China, the alliance likewise presents a strategic challenge. Sensitive to history, China is acutely focused on developments in Japan's security policy. In this context, the alliance generally has been treated as the lesser of two evils in that it has served to constrain movement in Japan toward "normalization"—the revision of its war-renouncing constitution and the exercise of the right of collective self-defense.

However, in mid-decade, Fudan University professor Wu Xinbo noted a transformation in Chinese thinking about the alliance—a shift from an appreciation of the alliance as a "useful constraint on Japan's remilitarization" toward the view that "enhanced security cooperation between Washington and Tokyo compromises China's security interests."[16] In this evolving context, Chinese analysts came to view U.S. policy—focused on balancing the rise of China and deterring China's possible use of forces against Taiwan—as now "driving rather than restraining Japan's rearmament." China is particularly sensitive to any indication that the alliance might be invoked to intervene in a Taiwan crisis. Japan's 1998 Defense Guidelines committed Japan to provide rear-area logistical support to U.S. forces in the event of contingencies "in areas surrounding Japan," and Beijing reacted strongly, expressing "grave concern" over the February 2005 "Two plus Two" joint statement in which Japan and the United States, reportedly at Japan's initiative, explicitly referred to the peaceful resolution of the Taiwan issue as one of their "common strategic objectives."[17]

Political Values

Postwar Japan has demonstrated a firm commitment to the democratic values enshrined it its constitution. Freedom of speech, freedom of assembly, freedom of the press, and freedom of religion are hallmarks of Japan's democracy. Their practice in Japan is also reflected in Japan's relations with China. In 2008, 2009, and 2010, internal developments in China became political issues in Japan and, in turn, affected the bilateral relationship.

Reacting to China's crackdown in Tibet in March 2008, the opposition Democratic Party of Japan pressed Prime Minister Yasuo Fukuda to raise the Tibet issue with President Hu Jintao during his visit to Japan and to consider a boycott of the Beijing Olympics. Democratic Party of Japan President Hatoyama said that it was important to send China a message that Tibet was a significant human rights issue; he called on Beijing to take the criticisms of the international community to heart and open a dialogue with the Dalai Lama. Japan's foreign minister asked Beijing to provide greater transparency regarding developments in Tibet, saying that Tibet was a human rights problem even if an internal affair of China's. Beijing's response was to blame the Dalai Lama and his supporters for rioting in an effort to sabotage the Beijing Olympics, again insisting that Tibet was an internal affair.

A year later, Japan granted a visa to Uighur activist Rebiya Kadeer. The decision drew strong protests from China. The Chinese foreign ministry called in the Japanese ambassador to express China's "strong dissatisfaction" for allowing Kadeer to visit Japan and engage in "anti-China separatist activities."[18] At the same time, China's ambassador to Japan charged Kadeer with being the leader of an organization that was responsible for rioting in Urumqi and emphasized the need for the two governments to address common interests, not be distracted by the actions of criminals.[19]

In November 2010, Foreign Minister Seiji Maehara told the Diet that China, following the award of the Nobel Peace Prize to detained dissident, Liu Xiabao, had asked Japan to refrain from having Japanese officials attend the award ceremony. At the political level, China's demarche found few supporters, and the government instructed its ambassador in Norway to attend the ceremony. Prime Minister Naoto Kan told the Diet that the Nobel was an expression of universal values and that Liu's release was desirable. At the public level, Japanese "netizens," reacting to Maehara's disclosure, characterized Beijing's demarche as an example of Chinese arrogance, called on China to stop abusing its own citizens, and asked what had happened to China's principle of noninterference in the domestic affairs of other countries.

While issues related to human rights and China's treatment of political dissidents and minorities are not likely to slow the movement of Japanese businesses to the mainland, the resonance of such issues across the Japanese body politic will continue to function as a structural impediment to efforts to deepen what most see as mutually beneficial strategic relationship. Unlike its values-based relationship with the United States, Japan's relations with China lack an enduring political foundation at the core of the relationship.

PART III: Case Studies

Managing Issues and the Relationship

Given the complex factors that shape the relationship, both governments are challenged with the day-to-day tasks of managing issues that, if left unaddressed, could negatively affect the bilateral relationship, despite the interest each side has in it, and complicate realization of the Mutually Beneficial Strategic Relationship. Issues such as history, food security, the East China Sea, and security may not lend themselves to resolution in the short- to midterm, but finding ways to deal with or work around the issues is necessary to keep the relationship on a more or less even keel and moving forward. Yet, as underscored by the Senkaku incident in September 2010, actions that touch national sensitivities and invite definition as zero-sum issues have the potential to derail the relationship at significant cost to both parties. The following case studies illuminate in different ways the challenges involved in managing this relationship both in Beijing and in Tokyo.

Shaping the Future, Managing the Past

In September 2006, Shinzo Abe succeeded Koizumi as President of the Liberal Democratic Party and Prime Minister. In his first policy speech to the Diet, Abe made clear his commitment to "strengthening bonds of trust" with China and South Korea.[20] On October 8, Abe, breaking a tradition of Japanese prime ministers traveling first to Washington, traveled instead to Beijing for an "ice-breaking" visit with China's leadership. In Beijing, the two sides in a joint press statement agreed to cooperate on a wide range of issues and to work to build a strategic, mutually beneficial relationship.

During a return "ice-melting" visit in April 2007, Premier Wen Jiabao addressed the Japanese Diet. In a speech televised in both countries, Wen acknowledged Japan's support and assistance in aiding China's modernization, declaring that "This is something the Chinese people

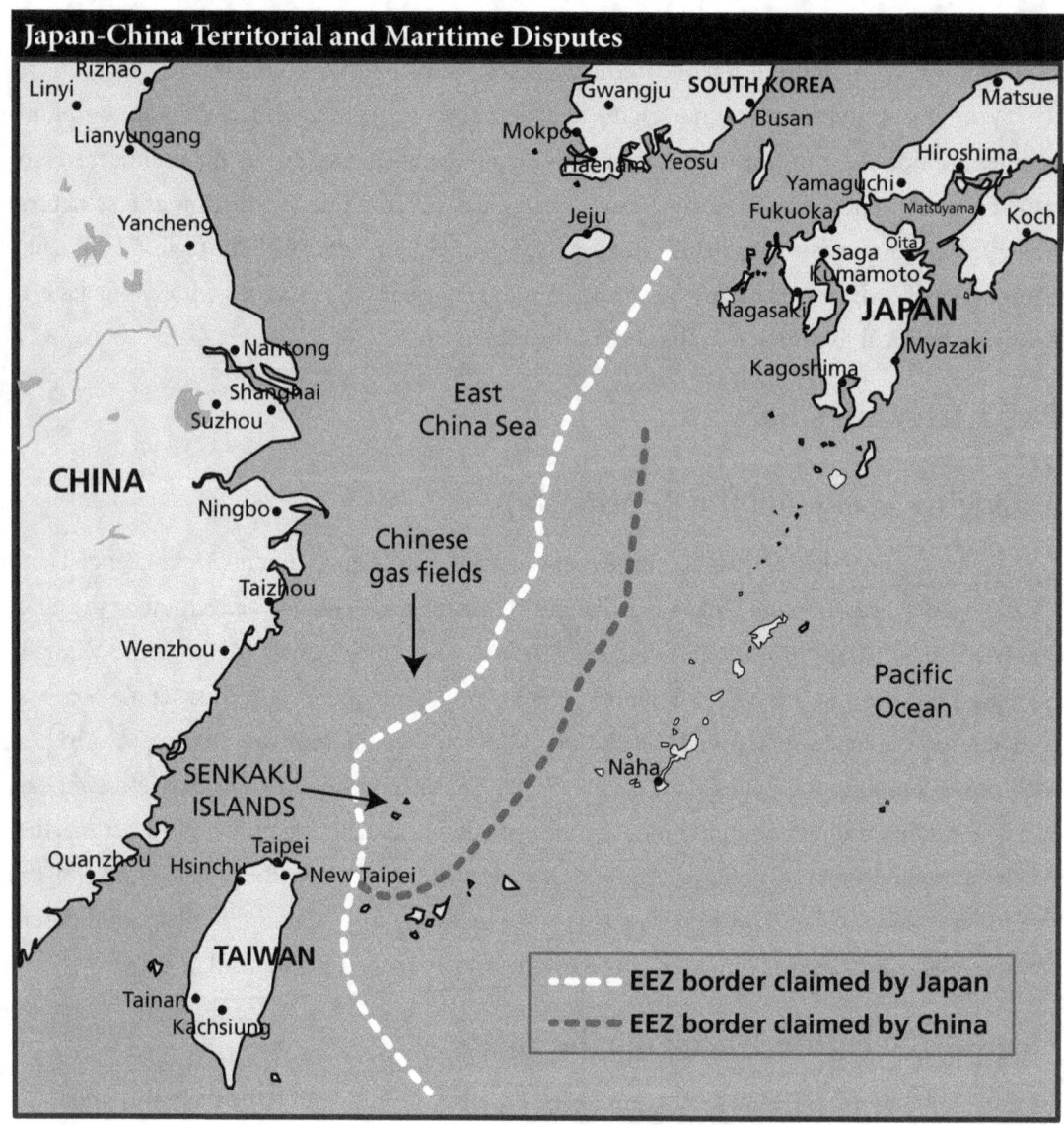

Japan-China Territorial and Maritime Disputes

will never forget." As for history, Wen put responsibility for the war on the shoulders of "a handful of militarists" and recognized that the Japanese people "were also victims of the war." He went on to say that China "positively evaluated" Japan's official recognition of its acts of aggression and its expression of "remorse and apology."[21] The joint press statement issued at the conclusion of the Wen visit reaffirmed "their common understanding on the building of a mutually beneficial relationship based on common strategic interests."[22]

Abe and Wen also agreed to a 3-year joint historical study. The study, completed in December 2009 and released at the end of January 2010, is divided into three historical periods:

ancient, medieval, and modern. Twenty-six papers were submitted, with half written by each side. The Japanese and Chinese papers, however, do not represent a consensus view of the past.

Japanese and Chinese scholars both used the word "aggression" with regard to the 1937–1945 Sino-Japanese war and the actions of the Imperial Army. The head of the Chinese team, Bu Ping, director of the Institute of Modern History at the Chinese Academy of Social Sciences, found the "common recognition and the issue of who bears responsibility for the war . . . is an important outcome."[23] As for the Marco Polo Bridge Incident, while many Chinese historians have consistently held the view that the action was "planned or plotted" by the Imperial Army, some Chinese contributors entertained "the possibility that it may have occurred accidentally." The two sides were unable to reach agreement on the number of deaths in Nanjing, and, at the request of China, the postwar section of the report, including the Tiananmen Square Massacre, was not made public.

Foreign Minister Katsuya Okada welcomed the reports, saying that "Even if there may be differences in views, especially in modern and contemporary history, I think a common understanding can gradually be nurtured by working on it."[24] Despite their differences, both Japanese and Chinese scholars recommended follow-on studies. An anonymous Japanese diplomat was quoted as observing that the study "was a smart mechanism in terms of managing bilateral relations in a smoother fashion."[25]

Yasukuni Shrine

Yasukuni Shrine, over the years, has come to embody the different understandings of modern history in China and Japan. Founded in 1869 by order of the Emperor Meiji, the shrine honors the spirits of Japan's war dead. At the end of World War II, the shrine, then viewed as a symbol of Japanese militarism, was removed from government administration and reestablished as a private religious corporation. In 1978, the spirits of 14 Class A war criminals were surreptitiously enshrined.[26]

The enshrinement of Class A war criminals and visits to the shrine by Japan's political leaders, particularly in an official capacity, have made Yasukuni a lightning rod in Japan-China relations. While a frequent visitor to Yasukuni before and after his term in office, Prime Minister Abe refrained from visiting the shrine as he worked to strengthen relations with China, but, in April 2009 during the spring festival, Prime Minister Aso presented the shrine with an offering of potted evergreen branches, making the gift an expression of his gratitude and respect for those who had given their lives for Japan.

China's foreign ministry initially took the relatively mild position that Yasukuni remained "an issue of major political sensitivity." No reference was made to a diplomatic protest.[27] Just 2 days later, however, the foreign ministry announced that China had already protested through diplomatic channels, expressing its "strong concern and dissatisfaction" and stressing "the high sensitivity of historical issues. The foreign ministry spokesperson, Jiang Yu, cautioned that any erroneous actions by Japan will have grave negative consequences for bilateral relations;" she went on, "we demand that the Japanese side exercise caution in its words and actions and appropriately deal with this." Finally, she stressed that a correct view and proper handling of historical issues constitutes the political foundation for sound and stable development of China-Japan relations; China hoped that Japan would act "so as to safeguard the overall interest of bilateral ties in a responsible manner."[28] Japanese media speculated that the announcement of the diplomatic protest and the stronger language of the second statement came in response to nationalistic reactions in China.

In 2010, Japan's new Prime Minister Naoto Kan announced that neither he nor members of his cabinet would visit Yasukuni Shrine on the August 15th anniversary of Japan's surrender. For the first time in nearly 30 years, not a single cabinet member of the Japanese government paid homage at the shrine. The issue, while dormant at present, is not departed.

Food Security

In early 2008, the safety of *gyoza* (dumplings) imported from China became a major political issue as reports of food poisoning suffered by Japanese consumers became front-page news.

Throughout 2008, the gyoza controversy generated mutual recriminations and finger-pointing over food-handling procedures and charges of irresponsible behavior as well as criminal misconduct by corporate and government officials.

In 2009, both governments acted to address the food safety issue. The Japan International Cooperation Agency hosted a 5-day conference in China devoted to strengthening China's inspection regime on food exports to Japan, while China's National People's Congress adopted legislation aimed at assuring food security. Later, Prime Minister Hatoyama and Premier Wen agreed to establish a bilateral consultation mechanism on food safety, subsequently agreeing to a memorandum of understanding on procedures to be followed in a future food security crisis, and signed a food safety agreement.

Nevertheless, the Japanese media greeted the 2010 anniversary of the gyoza incident with a sense of resignation that the controversy was unlikely to be resolved satisfactorily. However, at the end of March, Chinese authorities arrested a Chinese national, Lu Yueting, in connection with the incident. Under interrogation, Lu admitted to injecting the gyoza with a pesticide. Later, Chinese public security officials traveled to Tokyo to brief Japan's National Police Agency on the case. Prime Minister Hatoyama praised the efforts of the

Chinese authorities and expressed the hope that resolution of the incident would enhance bilateral relations.

Security/Confidence-building

At the 2006 Abe-Hu Summit, the two leaders agreed to resume vice ministerial–level defense talks in November 2006, after a hiatus of 18 months. In August, 2007, ministerial-level talks resumed after a 4-year hiatus with the visit of China's minister of defense to Japan. The defense ministers reached agreement on defense exchanges and reciprocal port calls as well as the development of a maritime communications mechanism between the two ministries. In November 2007, the PLA Navy destroyer *Shenzhen* docked at Harumi pier in Tokyo, marking the first visit of a PLA warship to Japan, and in June 2008, the Japanese Maritime Self-Defense Force destroyer *Sazanami* visited China, the first port call by a Japanese warship since 1945. Out of public safety concerns, Chinese authorities canceled a public concert that had been scheduled to celebrate the event.

At the same time, China's military modernization program is a cause of concern in Japan. In particular, the PLA Navy's stepped-up naval activities in the waters around Japan, aspirations for a blue-water navy, and the development of submarine and aircraft carrier capabilities have become a focus of Japanese media attention and raised security concerns in Japan. In early April 2010, a flotilla of 10 PLA Navy warships exercised in the East China Sea then transited international waters between Okinawa's main island and Miyakojima. The transit became front-page news in Tokyo and Defense Minister Toshimi Kitazawa characterized the size of the Chinese deployment as unprecedented in waters near Japan. On April 22, China's *International Herald Leader* noted Japanese nervousness but suggested that Japan should be prepared to adjust to increasingly frequent PLA Navy deployments.[29]

In response to the evolving security environment, Japan's National Defense Program Guidelines (NDPG), issued in December 2010, called for the development of "dynamic defense" capabilities that emphasize readiness, mobility, flexibility, sustainability, and versatility in order to respond to diverse contingencies. The strengthening of the Self-Defense Force's surveillance and warning capabilities is a priority. Among its missions, the SDF is to be prepared to ensure the security of the sea and air space surrounding Japan, to respond to attacks on offshore islands, and to respond to attacks by guerrillas and special operations forces. Highlighting increasing concerns with potential challenges to sovereignty in the distant southwest islands, the NDPG calls for the deployment of Ground Self-Defense Forces to these isolated locations. The new guidelines represent a significant change from the static defense posture that remained in effect 20 years after the end of the Cold War.[30]

Meanwhile, Chinese concerns have focused on the overseas deployments of Japan's Self-Defense Force in support of Operation *Iraqi Freedom*, on Japan's internal debate over constitutional revision and the exercise of the right of collective self-defense, and on the steps taken by Japan and the United States to strengthen their alliance. Beijing reacted negatively to the February 2005 "Two plus Two" joint statement, issued by the U.S.-Japan Security Consultative Committee, in which Japan and the United States, reportedly at Japan's initiative, explicitly referred to concerns about a peaceful resolution of the Taiwan issue.[31] Addressing the June 2011 "Two plus Two" joint statement, China's foreign minister expressed his government's "concern over the China-related issues raised by the U.S.-Japan military alliance."[32]

To address mutual security concerns, Tokyo and Beijing have conducted 12 rounds of Security Dialogues, involving senior foreign policy and defense officials. The most recent meeting took place in Beijing in January 2011, after a hiatus of almost 2 years. At the end of February 2011, the China-Japan Strategic Dialogue—suspended after the Senkaku incident—resumed in Tokyo.

East China Sea and Energy Development

In June 2008, after lengthy negotiations, Japan and China reached agreement on a joint development zone in the East China Sea. The agreement covered the Chunxiao/Shirakaba natural gas field as well as an area north-northeast of the field that straddles the midline boundary claimed by Japan. The agreement allows Japanese private sector companies as well as government-backed corporations to invest in the development of the existing Chunxiao/Shirakaba field. Excluded from the agreement were two areas then under development by China on its side of the median line as well as the area around the Senkaku Islands. Specifics regarding drilling locations, investment shares, and earning allocations were left for further negotiations. Both governments welcomed the deal as a sign that the two countries could work to resolve difficult issues, while agreeing that joint development would not prejudice existing boundary claims.

However, little progress has been made implementing negotiations. While Japan's political leadership has pressed Beijing to make the difficult political decisions necessary to implement the agreement, Chinese leaders and diplomats, concerned with a potential antigovernment, anti-Japanese nationalist backlash, have repeatedly pointed to the sensitive nature of the agreement and the need to prepare a proper environment for negotiations. However, in May 2010, China shifted its position and called for an early resumption of negotiations.

Talks resumed in July with agreement to meet again in September. On September 11, 2010, 4 days after a Chinese fishing trawler collided with two Japanese coast guard ships, the Chinese foreign ministry announced postponement of the September talks in response to Japan's detention of the captain and crew of the trawler. Efforts to restart the talks at a meeting of Japanese and Chinese foreign ministers on the sidelines of the November 2010 Asia-Pacific Economic Cooperation (APEC) meeting in Yokohama proved unavailing.

Senkaku Breakdown

On September 7, 2010, a Chinese fishing trawler collided with two Japanese coast guard ships north of the Senkaku Islands and within Japan's claimed EEZ. The coast guard ships pursued and boarded the Chinese trawler, taking the captain and crew into custody. The rapid deterioration of relations that followed underscored the enduring strength of the structural constraints that mark the China-Japan relationship.

The coast guard remanded the captain to prosecutors for investigation and a decision on indictment for obstructing the coast guard in the execution of its lawful duties.[33] Prime Minister Kan took the position that Japan's actions were strictly correct, based on Japanese law, and in Japanese waters. Beijing's immediate response was to call for Japan to refrain from taking "so-called law enforcement activities" in Chinese waters.[34] To accept the legality of the coast guard's action would compromise China's claim to sovereignty over the islands.

Beijing called for the immediate release of the captain, crew, and boat "to avoid further escalation"; pointed to the "highly sensitive" nature of territorial and sovereignty issues; cautioned that "improper handling of which will have a serious impact on the overall interest of China-Japan relations; and warned that "Japan should have a clear understanding of that."[35] Japanese authorities released the crew and ship but extended the captain's detention.[36] Reacting to the continuing detention, Beijing accused Japan of not only provoking the situation but of "doubling its mistakes, causing further escalation" and made clear that "if Japan obstinately clings to its course, it must shoulder all responsibilities." Stepping up pressure, Beijing ruled out a Kan-Wen meeting during the UN General Assembly meeting in New York, suspended all ministerial and high-level exchanges with Tokyo, and cautioned China's tourist industry against travel to Japan.[37]

In remarks to Chinese nationals and Chinese-Americans in New York, Premier Wen called for the immediate release of the captain and made clear that Japan "bears full responsibility for the situation, and it will bear all the consequences."[38] Wen told his audience, "The Japanese side has paid no heed to China's numerous serious representations, and so China cannot take necessary countermeasures and warned that "If Japan acts willfully despite advice to the contrary, China will take further actions, and Japan must accept full responsibility for all the severe consequences."[39] On September 23, the *New York Times* reported that China was moving to cut rare earth metal exports to Japan to build pressure on the Japanese business community and, in turn, on the government for a resolution of the issue.

Japanese prosecutors released the captain on September 25. China responded by demanding an apology and compensation for the illegal detention, reiterating that the Diaoyu Islands have been part of China's territory "since ancient times" and accusing Japan of actions that "seriously violated China's territorial sovereignty and the human rights of the Chinese nationals."[40]

Anti-Japanese protests spread through China in mid-October and were followed by smaller scale anti-Chinese protests in Japan. Efforts by diplomats to restart the Mutually Beneficial Strategic Relationship ran into strong political headwinds when video of the September 7 collisions, which clearly showed the Chinese trawler running into Japan's coast guard ships, was publicly uploaded to YouTube. Prime Minster Kan did meet with China's leadership during the Asia-Europe Meeting and the East Asia Summit meetings in October and during the APEC meeting in November. But the Kan-Wen and the Kan-Hu meetings were hotel lobby or corridor meet-and-greets, with the Chinese taking care to emphasize the informal, conversational nature of the encounters.[41]

National Fallout

On September 20, in the wake of the Senkaku fishing boat incident, the daily newspaper *Sankei Shimbun* and the Fuji News Network conducted a spot public opinion survey. Of the respondents, 79.7 percent answered that their image of China had worsened, while 71.5 percent found China to be a threat to Japan's national security. Only 7 percent found China to be trustworthy; in stark contrast, 85.1 percent said that China was not trustworthy. Meanwhile, 86.8 percent recognized that China was important for Japan's economic well-being. Support for the Kan government fell from 64.2 percent in a previous mid-September survey to 48.5 percent, with 78.8 percent of respondents citing concerns with the government's handling of the fishing boat incident.[42]

A *Yomiuri Shimbun* telephone survey conducted October 1–3 tracked closely with the Fuji-Sankei poll. In the *Yomiuri* survey, 84 percent of respondents said they did not trust China, surpassing the previous high of 77 percent in a 2008 survey. At the same time, 72 percent said that the government's release of the fishing boat captain was not appropriate, citing the appearance that Japan had caved into pressure as the reason, and 94 percent found China's demand for an apology and compensation "unconvincing." Looking ahead, 90 percent of the respondents called on the government to assert its position more forcefully on the Senkakus and 71 percent called on the government to strengthen its alliance with the United States.

The downward trend continued. Released on November 2, a Fuji-Sankei poll found 86.6 percent of respondents saying they could not trust China, up 3.5 percent from September; only 6.4 percent could trust China. Moreover, in a joint Yomiuri-China News Agency telephone poll released on November 8, 90 percent of Japanese respondents said that bilateral relations are in bad shape and 87 percent said they could not trust China. In China, 81 percent of respondents said relations were in bad shape, and 79 percent said they could not trust Japan.[43]

On December 18, the cabinet office released results of its annual public opinion poll on Japan's foreign relations. Questionnaires were sent to 3,000 adults; the survey had a 65 percent response rate. Of the respondents, 88.6 percent did not perceive relations with China to be good, an increase of 33.4 percent over 2009 and the highest percentage since 1986; 77.8 percent did not feel affinity toward China, an increase of 19.3 percent and the highest since 1978 when the survey was first conducted. Only 18.5 percent held affinity toward China, a decrease of 20 percent; and only 8.3 percent thought relations with China to be in good shape, a drop of 30.2 percent. A Yomiuri-Gallup poll released on December 22 confirmed the cabinet office findings. Only 8 percent of respondents trusted China, while those who did not trust China "very much" stood at 47 percent and "not at all" represented 40 percent.[44] The rising degree of public mistrust in both countries highlights the difficult environment with which political leaders and diplomats will have to contend in managing the relationship.

Managing Issues: An Assessment

The case studies considered above illuminate the day-to-day challenges involved in managing this complex and multidimensional relationship. Some issues have been resolved successfully, while some are being managed and kept under control, while still others speak to underlying centrifugal forces in this relationship.

Resolution of the gyoza/food safety controversy was an unqualified success. Despite the inflamed media discourse in both China and Japan, officials in both countries were able to solve the gyoza case and advance cooperation on food safety issues. Likewise, the Joint Study of History project, while not producing mutual agreement on the sensitive issues of the 1920s and 1930s, did at least serve to narrow the gaps in understanding, and the Yasukuni issue has been set aside for the moment.

The 2008 agreement on the joint development of the East China Sea reflects recognition both in Beijing and in Tokyo of the critical economic component at the core of the bilateral relationship and the mutual benefit to be derived from economic cooperation. However, efforts to implement the agreement have been subject to nationalist reactions to reported negotiating concessions and to political developments outside the economic sphere, the latest being the Senkaku incident, which led China to suspend negotiations. As of this writing, the two sides have yet to agree to resume talks. That the two governments have not disavowed the agreement represents a victory for muddling through.

China's military modernization program and the PLA Navy's increasing operations in international waters around Japan is now part of Japan's public discourse and political debate. Japan's response has been to strengthen its alliance relationship with the United States and to engage China in security and strategic dialogues. However, it is not evident that the Japan-China defense and security confidence-building measures have slowed the pace of PLA modernization or naval operations, but they do demonstrate a commitment of both parties to continue to manage security issues and keep them from enflaming the relationship.

Meanwhile, territorial and sovereignty issues are the "third rail" of the relationship and, as highlighted by the Senkaku incident, have the potential to bring it to a full stop across the board. They are binary win-lose issues on which political compromise is exceedingly difficult under the best of circumstances. In the case of China and Japan, history and nationalism remain powerful, latent forces coursing through their relationship. Set against such forces, issues related to sovereignty, security, and even economics become intricately complex and challenging to political leaders and diplomats in both countries. Once issues are caught up in this powerful undertow, enduring solutions are difficult to advance.

Efforts will be made to right the ship and move on. At the June 2011 Shangri-la dialogue in Singapore, Chinese and Japanese ministers of defense agreed to resume defense exchanges at the earliest appropriate time and, in July, Chinese and Japanese foreign ministers met in Beijing for the first time in almost 11 months. But, notwithstanding the mutual economic benefits that drive and are derived from this relationship, the China-Japan relationship will continue to be subject to deep political and security crosscurrents.

As a result, Japan will look to the alliance with the United States to help manage the security risks involved in its relations with China and will be concerned with any signs of U.S. retreat from Asia or diminished U.S. capabilities in the region.

Conclusion

Since the advent of the Abe government, both Tokyo and Beijing have worked to stabilize bilateral relations. Within the framework of the Mutually Beneficial Strategic Relationship, the two governments have endeavored to manage or work around day-to-day issues—the East China Sea, food safety, security issues, human rights, as well as the always present past—even as both attempt to deal with evolving geostrategic realities, the rise of China, and competition for influence in the Asia-Pacific region and beyond.

Japan's active engagement with China is reflected particularly in cultural and economic affairs. Japan has eased visa requirements for individual Chinese tourists, and the rapid increase in Chinese tourists is encouraging as the two governments work to build people-to-people ties. Moreover, in the absence of a significant downturn in relations, Japanese companies, following a long-term trajectory, will be focused increasingly on the China market. Underscoring the economic imperatives driving Japan's engagement with China, Prime Minister Kan appointed Japan's first nonforeign service ambassador to China, Uichiro Niwa, former chairman of trading giant Itochu Corporation, long a leading player in the China market.

Nevertheless, China's ongoing military buildup and the PLA Navy's increasing operations in waters off Japan have heightened Japanese security concerns and are affecting the evolution of Japan's security policy. Japan's new NDPG, issued in December 2010, and the first China Security report, issued in March 2011, by the National Institute for Defense Studies, underscore themes of continuing concern—China's modernization of air, naval, nuclear, and missile forces; its development of power projection capabilities; lack of transparency; and increasing maritime activities.

Despite the efforts of both governments, political relations remain fragile and volatile. After the Senkaku incident, China broke off all high-level political and diplomatic contact and used its economic leverage on Japan's private sector as part of a full-court press to secure its diplomatic objective. Polling data in Japan at the end of 2010 portend a difficult political future, even as both governments seek to expand economic ties and advance the Mutually Beneficial Strategic Relationship.

Implications for the United States

For the United States, keeping a proper balance between China and Japan, as Beijing and Tokyo work through their own complicated relations, will challenge U.S. diplomacy at a time when Washington has important regional and global interests to pursue with both countries. The communiqué released at the U.S.-China Summit in January 2011 makes clear the multifaceted nature of the U.S. engagement with China and the significant national interests at stake. Similarly, the joint statement issued at the conclusion of the U.S.-Japan "Two plus Two" meeting in June underscores the broad scope of international interests and concerns shared by the two allies and highlights their mutual commitment to cooperate in addressing international challenges.

For over 30 years, the United States and Japan have pursued remarkably similar policies toward China. Seeing a prosperous China as a stable China, they have worked to support the economic opening and reforms initiated by Deng Xiaoping. To this end, they actively supported

China's admission into the World Trade Organization. Moreover, they have encouraged China to become the "Responsible Stakeholder" envisaged by Robert Zoellick in terms of China's role in the international system. Across-the-board engagement defines the strategy of both countries toward China.

Yet both countries face the challenge of managing risk in their relations with China. For example, what if their engagement strategies prove inadequate or what if China develops in a trajectory different from the one hoped for by the United States and Japan? For both countries, the answer to the risk management questions has been to strengthen the values-based U.S.-Japan alliance to protect their respective interests in Asia and beyond and, at the same time, to "encourage China's responsible and constructive role in regional stability and prosperity, its cooperation on global issues, and its adherence to international norms of behavior." For both Washington and Tokyo, the alliance is a vital national interest.[45]

Recognizing that the U.S.-Japan Security Alliance has served as the foundation for stability in the Asia-Pacific region for over 50 years and is a pillar of U.S. global strategy should be the starting point in developing a comprehensive policy approach to both Beijing and Tokyo. A Japan confident in its security is a Japan that can more confidently engage China to its benefit, to the benefit of China, and to the benefit of the Asia-Pacific region.

Notes

[1] The Oxford English Dictionary defines *meta* as a prefix and or preposition whose "chief senses are: sharing, action in common; pursuit or quest: and esp. change (of place, order, condition or nature)." It is with reference to change of place, order, condition or nature, that I use the word in this article.

[2] Chih-Yu Shih, "Defining Japan: The Nationalist Assumption in China's Foreign Policy," *International Journal* 50, no. 3 (Summer 1995), 543–544.

[3] Erica Strecker Downs and Phillip C. Saunders, "Legitimacy and the Limits of Nationalism: China and the Daioyu Islands, *International Security* 23, no. 3, Winter 1998–1999.

[4] See Suisheng Zhao, "China's Pragmatic Nationalism: Is it Manageable?" *The Washington Quarterly* 29, no. 1 (Winter 2005–2006), 131–144. In response to the anti-Japanese riots of 2005, Japanese investors began to hedge their bets by adopting a "China plus one" strategy, pairing investments in China with investments in various Association of Southeast Asian Nations (ASEAN) countries to limit their dependence on China. In 2006, Japanese companies invested more in ASEAN than it did in China, reversing the trend of previous years.

[5] Premier Wen Jiabao, in his April 12, 2007, speech to the Japanese Diet, televised in both countries, acknowledged Japan's support and assistance in aiding China's opening, reform, and modernization, declaring that "This is something the Chinese people will never forget." China's leadership also thanked Japan for its relief efforts in the aftermath of the 2008 Chengdu earthquake.

[6] Kyodo News International, "Japan-China Joint History Research Highlights Gap in Views," *Japan Today*, December 30, 2009, available at <www.istockanalyst.com/article/viewiStockNews/articleid/3738551>.

[7] See Taro Aso, minister for foreign affairs, speech on the occasion of the Japan Institute of International Affairs seminar, "Arc of Freedom and Prosperity: Japan's Expanding Diplomatic Horizons," November 30, 2006, available at <www.mofa.go.jp/announce/fm/aso/speech0611.html>.

[8] See "China's Lee Tells African Officials G-5 Plan against UN Solidarity," Japan Economic Newswire, June 6, 2005; and "China Supports African Union Stance on UN Security Council Reform," BBC Monitoring Asia Pacific—Political, August 6, 2005.

[9] Position Paper of the People's Republic of China at the 65th Session of the United Nations General Assembly, September 13, 2010, available at <www.fmprc.gov.cn.eng/zxxx/t751986.htm>; on December 1, 2010, the *Yomiuri Shimbun*, drawing on the Wikileaks Web site, reported that in April of 2009, China's vice foreign minister, speaking to the issue of United Nation Security Council reform, told a U.S. diplomat that "It is difficult for the Chinese people to accept Japan as a permanent member."

[10] Joseph Khan, "China Is Pushing and Scripting Anti-Japanese Protests," *The New York Times*, April 15, 2005, available at <www.nytimes.com/2005/04/15/international/asia/15china.html?_r=1&pagewanted=1>.

[11] International Monetary Fund (IMF), *Direction of Trade Statistics Yearbook 2001* (Washington, DC: IMF), 277; and IMF, *Direction of Trade Statistics Yearbook 2011* (Washington, DC: IMF 2011), 305.

[12] Chico Harlan, "Anxiety over Japanese Economy Deepens after Grim Reports," *The Washington Post* (August 27, 2010), A15.

[13] "Aso, Wen Clash over Disputed Islands during Talks as PRC Steps Up Offensive," *Asahi Shimbun* [in Japanese], OSC Translation JPP20081215036002, December 13, 2008.

[14] Ibid.

[15] In recent years, Japan's defense spending has been actually less than 1 percent.

[16] Wu Xinbo, "The End of the Silver Lining: A Chinese View of the U.S.-Japan Alliance," *The Washington Quarterly* 29, no. 1 (Winter 2005–2006), 119–130.

[17] Xinhuanet News Agency, "Beijing Opposes U.S.-Japan Statement on Taiwan," *China View*, February 20, 2005, available at <http://news.xinhuanet.com/english/2005-02/20/content_2596291.htm>.

[18] Xinhuanet News Agency, "Rebiya's Visit to Japan Will Spell Trouble for China-Japan Relations: Chinese Ambassador," *China View*, July 29, 2009, available at <http://news.xinhuanet.com/english/2009-07/29/content_11790330.htm>.

[19] "Uyghur Leader Rebiya Kadeer in Japan, Beijing Protests," Asia News, April 13, 2012, available at <www.asianews.it/index.php?1=en&art=15900&size=A>.

[20] Shinzo Abe, press conference, September 26, 2006, available at <www.kantei.go.jp/foreign/abespeech/2006/09/26press_e.html>; During the Junichiro Koizumi years (2001–2006), the prime minister's visits to the Yasukuni Shrine aggravated tensions in Sino-Japanese relations. In protest, China suspended high-level contacts with Japan's political leadership.

[21] Tomiichi Murayama, statement, "On the Occasion of the 50th Anniversary of the War's End," August 15, 1995, available at <www.mofa.go.jp/announce/press/pm/murayama/9508.html>. On August 15, 1995, Prime Minister Tomiichi Murayama issued a statement that acknowledged that Japan, "through its colonial rule and aggression, caused tremendous damage and suffering to the people of many countries, particularly to those of Asian nations. In the hope that no such mistake be made in the future, I regard, in a spirit of humility, these irrefutable facts and express here once again my feelings of deep remorse and state my heartfelt apology." Successive Japanese governments have reaffirmed the Murayama statement.

[22] Ministry of Foreign Affairs of Japan, Tokyo, "Japan-China Joint Press Statement (provisional translation)," April 11, 2007, available at <www.mofa.go.jp/region/asia-paci/china/pv0704/joint.html>.

[23] Ko Hirano, "Japan-China History Report to Break New Ground," Kyodo News, *The Japan Times*, January 21, 2010, available at <www.japantimes.co.jp/text/nn20100121f1.html>.

[24] Kyodo News, "Japan, China Still at Odds over Nanjing," *The Japan Times*, February 1, 2010, available at <www.japantimes.co.jp/text/nn20100201a1.html>.

[25] Hirano.

[26] Following World War II, the Allied countries indicted 28 of Japan's wartime government and military leaders for war crimes. Of those indicted, 25 were convicted of Class A War Crimes by the International Military Tribunal for the Far East 1946–1948; among them, 14 were enshrined at Yasukuni.

[27] "Foreign Ministry Spokesperson Jiang Yu's Regular Press Conference," April 21, 2009, available at <www.fmprc.gov.cn/eng/xwfw/s2510/t558550.htm>.

[28] "Foreign Ministry Spokesperson Jiang Yu's Regular Press Conference," April 23, 2009, available at <www.fmprc.gov.cn/eng/xwfw/s2510/t558968.htm>; and Edward Young, "Japan Shrine Offering Angers China," *The New York Times*, April 23, 2009.

[29] James J. Przystup, "Japan-China Relations: Troubled Waters to Calm Seas?" *Comparative Connections* 12, no. 2, July 2010.

[30] See Japan, Ministry of Defense, "National Defense Program Guidelines," December 17, 2010, available at <www.mod.go.jp/e/d_act/d_policy/national.html>.

[31] The U.S.-Japan Security Consultative Committee is composed of the U.S. Secretaries of State and Defense and Japan's Ministers of Foreign Affairs and Defense. The Committee meets as necessary to address alliance issues; there are no regularly scheduled meetings.

[32] Ministry of Foreign Affairs of the People's Republic of China, "Yang Jiechi Holds Talks with Japanese Foreign Minister Takeaki Matsumoto," July 5, 2011, available at <www.fmprc.gov.cn/eng/zxxx/t837140.htm>.

[33] In previous incursions, Tokyo had simply expelled the intruders; in this case, the government viewed the collision as obstructing official coast guard activities and thus a violation of Japanese law. The reference to Japanese law highlighted the issue of Japanese sovereignty over the Senkakus, which Beijing could not accept.

[34] "Foreign Ministry Spokesperson Jiang Yu's Regular Press Conference," September 7, 2010, available at <http://si.chineseembassy.org/eng/fyrth/t738694.htm>.

[35] "Foreign Ministry Spokesperson Jiang Yu's Regular Press Conference," September 9, 2010, available at <http://gd.china-embassy.org/eng/fyrth/t739264.htm>.

[36] On September 20, 2010, Chinese authorities detained four Japanese employees of the Fujita Corporation for allegedly entering without permission a military zone in Hebei Province and taking unauthorized photographs and videos; the last of the four Fujita employees was released on October 9, 2010.

[37] Agence France-Presse, "Clinton Says Disputed Islands Part of Japan-U.S. Pact: Maehara," *Energy Daily*, September 24, 2010, available at <www.energy-daily.com/reports/Clinton-says-disputed islands_part_of_Japan-US_pact_Maehara_999.html>. Secretary of State Hillary Clinton and Foreign Minister Seiji Maehara met in New York City on September 23, 2010. Following the meeting, Maehara told reporters that the Secretary of State had given assurances that Article V of the Security Treaty extended to the Senkakus. Moreover, during a joint press conference with Maehara on October 27 in Honolulu, Hawaii, Secretary Clinton again announced that the Security Treaty applied to the Senkakus; Department of State, Joint Press Availability, October 27, 2010, available at <www.state.gov/secretary/rm/2010/10/150110.htm>.

[38] Peter Foster, "China's Premier Ratchets up Pressure on Japan in Diplomatic Dispute," *The Telegraph*, September 22, 2010, available at <www.telegraph.co.uk/news/worldnews/asia/china/8018090/Chinas-premier-ratchets-up-pressure-on-Japan-in-diplomatic-dispute.html>.

[39] Tania Branigan and Justin McCurry, "China Prime Minister Demands Captain's Release," *The Guardian*, September 22, 2010, available at <www.guardian.co.uk/world/2010/sep/22/china-demands-captain-release>.

[40] "Foreign Ministry Spokesperson Jiang Yu's Remarks," September 25, 2010, available at <http://fm.China-embassy.org/eng/fyrth/t756293.htm>.

[41] In a January 2011 meeting with the author, members of the Democratic Party of Japan (DPJ) attributed the downturn in relations that followed the Senkaku incident to a number of communication problems: between China's foreign ministry and the Japanese embassy; between the Japanese embassy

and the foreign ministry in Tokyo; and between the DPJ's political leadership and Japanese bureaucrats; as well as the lack of an effective political back-channel between Tokyo and Beijing.

[42] James J. Przystup, "Japan-China Relations: Troubled Waters to Calm Seas?" *Comparative Connections* 12, no. 4, January 2011.

[43] Ibid.

[44] Ibid.

[45] U.S. Department of State, "Toward a Deeper and Broader U.S.-Japan Alliance: Building on 50 Years of Partnership," Joint Statement of the U.S.-Japan Security Consultative Committee, Washington, DC, June 21, 2011, available at <www.state.gov/r/pa/prs/ps/2011/06/166597.htm>.

About the Author

James J. Przystup, Ph.D., is a Senior Research Fellow in the Center for Strategic Research, Institute for National Strategic Studies, at the National Defense University. Dr. Przystup has worked on issues related to East Asia for close to 30 years on Capitol Hill, on the House of Representatives Subcommittee on Asian and Pacific Affairs, as the Deputy Director of the Presidential Commission on U.S.-Japan Relations, in the private sector at IBM, on the Policy Planning Staff of the Department of State, in the Office of the Secretary of Defense, and as Director of the Asian Studies Center at The Heritage Foundation. He holds a B.A. Summa Cum Laude from the University of Detroit and an M.A. and Ph.D. from the University of Chicago.

www.ingramcontent.com/pod-product-compliance
Lightning Source LLC
Chambersburg PA
CBHW080752290526
45790CB00008B/3422